Pebble® Plus
Bilingüe/ Bilingual

La Tierra en acción/Earth in Action

Huracanes/Hurricanes

por/by Mari Schuh

Editora consultora/Consulting Editor: Gail Saunders-Smith, PhD

Consultora/Consultant: Susan L. Cutter, PhD
Distinguida Profesora y Directora de Carolina/Carolina Distinguished Professor and Director
Instituto de Investigación de Peligros y Vulnerabilidad/Hazards & Vulnerability Research Institute
Departamento de Geografía/Department of Geography
University of South Carolina

CAPSTONE PRESS
a capstone imprint

Pebble Plus is published by Capstone Press,
151 Good Counsel Drive, P.O. Box 669, Mankato, Minnesota 56002.
www.capstonepub.com

 Books published by Capstone Press are manufactured with paper
containing at least 10 percent post-consumer waste.

Library of Congress Cataloging-in-Publication Data
Schuh, Mari C., 1975–
    [Hurricanes. Spanish & English]
    Huracanes = Hurricanes / por Mari Schuh.
    p. cm.—(Pebble Plus bilingüe. La tierra en acción = Pebble Plus bilingual. Earth in action)
    Summary: "Describes hurricanes, how they form, and the damage they cause—in both English and Spanish"—
Provided by publisher.
    Includes index.
    ISBN 978-1-4296-5356-5 (library binding)
    1. Hurricanes—Juvenile literature. I. Title. II. Title: Hurricanes. III. Series.
QC944.2.S3818 2011
551.55'2—dc22   2010004992

Editorial Credits
Erika L. Shores, editor; Strictly Spanish, translation services; Lori Bye, set designer; Wanda Winch, media researcher;
    Eric Manske and Danielle Ceminsky, designers; Laura Manthe, production specialist

Photo Credits
AP Images/St. Petersburg Times/Douglas R. Clifford, 5
Art Life Images/Jeff Greenberg, 13
Capstone Press/Karon Dubke, 19
Comstock Images, 1
FEMA News Photo/Robert Kaufmann, 21
Getty Images Inc./AFP/NOAA/HO, 15; James Nielsen, 17
Photodisc, cover
Shutterstock/Vladislav Gurfinkel, 11; Yury Zaporozhchenko, 7
Zuma Press/Lonely Planet Images/Wade Eakle, 9

Note to Parents and Teachers

The La Tierra en acción/Earth in Action set supports national science standards related to earth
science. This book describes and illustrates hurricanes in both English and Spanish. The images
support early readers in understanding the text. The repetition of words and phrases helps early
readers learn new words. This book also introduces early readers to subject-specific vocabulary
words, which are defined in the Glossary section. Early readers may need assistance to read
some words and to use the Table of Contents, Glossary, Internet Sites, and Index sections of
the book.

Printed in the United States of America, North Mankato, MN
072011
006231CGVMI

Table of Contents

Tabla de contenidos

What Is a Hurricane?

Hurricanes are huge, strong ocean storms. They can bring big waves, strong wind, and heavy rain to shore.

¿Qué es un huracán?

Los huracanes son tormentas enormes y fuertes en el océano. Ellos pueden traer olas grandes, vientos fuertes y mucha lluvia a la costa.

Hurricanes often happen
in summer and fall.
They form over
warm, tropical ocean water.

Los huracanes ocurren a menudo
en el verano y el otoño.
Ellos se forman sobre aguas
oceánicas templadas y tropicales.

How Hurricanes Form

Above warm oceans,
wet air rises. Wind starts to
blow hard. Wind and rain
form many thunderstorms.

Cómo se forman los huracanes

Un aire húmedo se eleva sobre los
océanos templados. El viento comienza
a soplar fuertemente. El viento y la lluvia
forman muchas tormentas eléctricas.

The thunderstorms come together
in a spinning circle. The storm gets
bigger. The middle of the storm
circle is called the eye.

Las tormentas eléctricas se juntan
en un círculo que gira. La tormenta
crece. El centro del círculo de
la tormenta se llama el ojo.

eye/ ojo

Learning about Hurricanes

Meteorologists use satellites

and radar to show

a hurricane's path.

Aprende sobre los huracanes

Los meteorólogos usan satélites

y radares para mostrar

el camino del huracán.

Hurricane hunters fly airplanes into the hurricane. They measure the storm's wind speed, temperature, and pressure.

Los cazadores de huracanes vuelan aviones dentro del huracán. Ellos miden la velocidad del viento, la temperatura y la presión de la tormenta.

A hurricane's strength is measured
by its wind speed. It is given
a number from one to five
on the Saffir-Simpson scale.

La fuerza de un huracán se mide
por la velocidad de su viento.
Se le da un número de uno a cinco
en la escala Saffir-Simpson.

Staying Safe

Prepare for a hurricane if you live near the coast. Pack food, water, and supplies. Stay inside and listen for reports on the radio.

Cómo permanecer seguro

Prepárate para un huracán si vives cerca de la costa. Almacena comida, agua y suministros. Permanece adentro y escucha los reportes en la radio.

After a Hurricane

Hurricanes can destroy towns

with wind and floods.

It takes a long time

for people to rebuild.

Después de un huracán

Los huracanes pueden destruir

pueblos con vientos e inundaciones.

Les lleva mucho tiempo a

las personas reconstruir.

Glossary

hurricane—a strong, swirling wind and rain storm that starts on the ocean; hurricanes are also called typhoons or cyclones

meteorologist—a person who studies and predicts the weather

pressure—a force that pushes on something

radar—a weather tool that sends out microwaves to determine the size, strength, and movement of storms

Saffir-Simpson scale—a scale from one to five that rates a hurricane based on its wind speed; the scale helps experts guess how much damage and flooding the hurricane might cause

satellite—a machine circling Earth that gathers information

tropical—having to do with the hot and wet areas near the equator

Internet Sites

FactHound offers a safe, fun way to find Internet sites related to this book. All of the sites on FactHound have been researched by our staff.

Here's all you do:

Visit *www.facthound.com*

Type in this code: 9781429653565

Glosario

la escala Saffir-Simpson—una escala de uno a cinco que categoriza a un huracán basado en la velocidad de su viento; la escala ayuda a los expertos a estimar cuánto daño e inundación puede causar el huracán

el huracán—una tormenta con vientos y lluvias fuertes en el océano; los huracanes también se llaman tifones o ciclones

el meteorólogo—una persona que estudia y predice el tiempo

la presión—una fuerza que empuja algo

el radar—una herramienta meteorológica que envía microondas para determinar el tamaño, la fuerza y el movimiento de las tormentas

el satélite—un equipo que circula la Tierra para juntar información

tropical—relacionado a áreas calurosas y húmedas cerca del ecuador

Sitios de Internet

FactHound brinda una forma segura y divertida de encontrar sitios de Internet relacionados con este libro. Todos los sitios en FactHound han sido investigados por nuestro personal.

Esto es todo lo que tienes que hacer:

Visita *www.facthound.com*

Ingresa este código: 9781429653565

Index

Índice